LET'S LOOK AT FEELINGS™

What I Look Like When I Am Sad

Joanne Randolph

The Rosen Publishing Group's
PowerStart Press™
New York

Published in 2004 by The Rosen Publishing Group, Inc.
29 East 21st Street, New York, NY 10010

First Edition

Book Design: Kim Sonsky

Photo Credits: All photographs by Maura B. McConnell.

Library of Congress Cataloging-in-Publication Data

Randolph, Joanne.
What I look like when I am sad / Joanne Randolph.— 1st ed.
    p. cm. — (Let's look at feelings)
Summary: Describes what different parts of a face look like when a person is sad.
Includes bibliographical references and index.
ISBN 1-4042-2507-2 (library binding)
1. Sadness in children—Juvenile literature. [1. Sadness. 2. Facial expression. 3. Emotions.] I.
Title. II. Series.
BF723.S15R36 2004
152.4—dc21

                                    2003009072

Manufactured in the United States of America

2

Contents

I am sad.

5

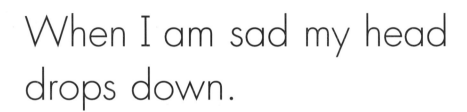

When I am sad my head drops down.

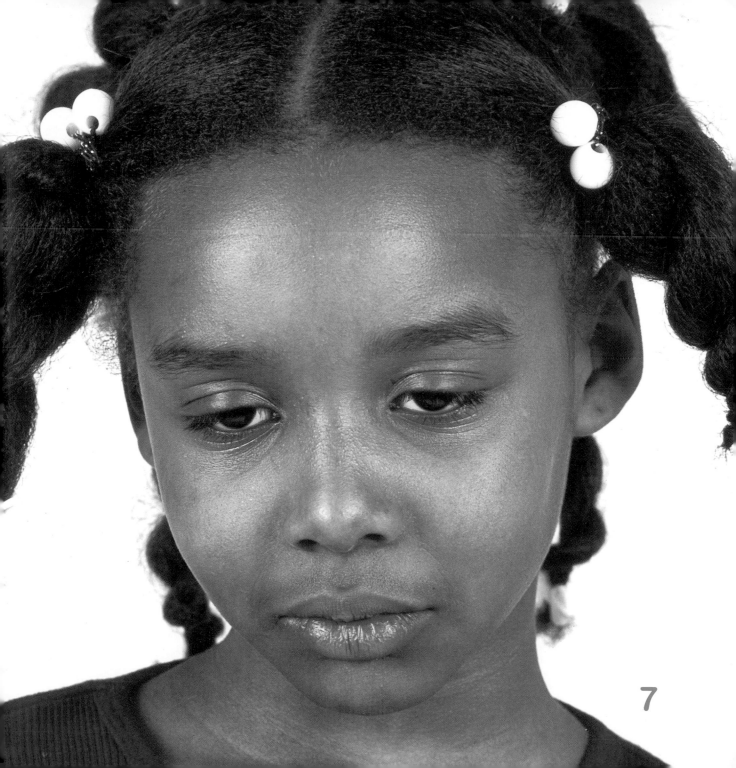

7

When I am sad my mouth makes a frown.

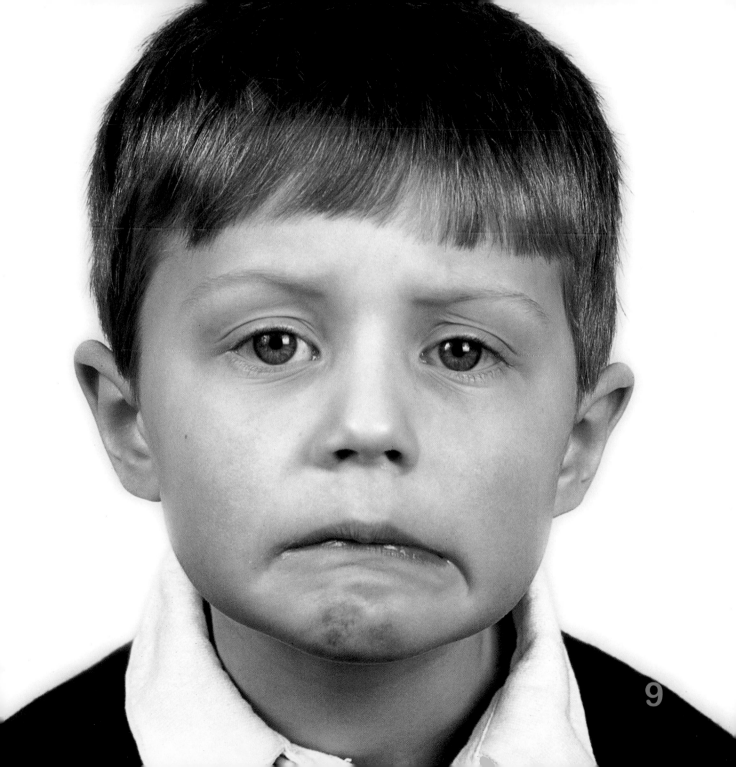

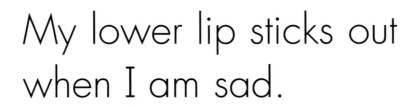

My lower lip sticks out
when I am sad.

11

When I am sad my
eyebrows wrinkle.

13

My eyes look down
when I am sad.

14

When I am sad my eyelids close.

When I am very sad I cry.

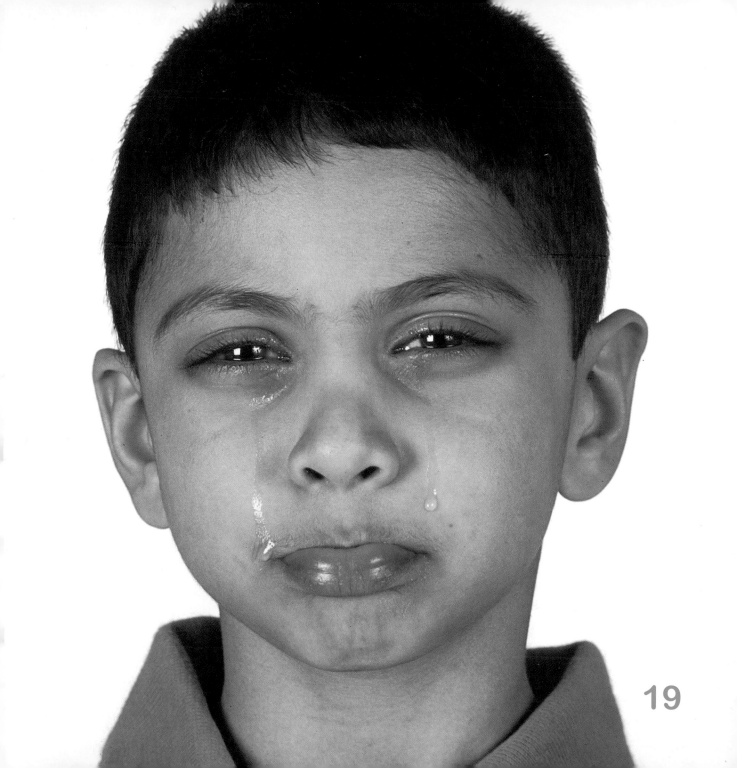

19

My eyes look red when I am very sad.

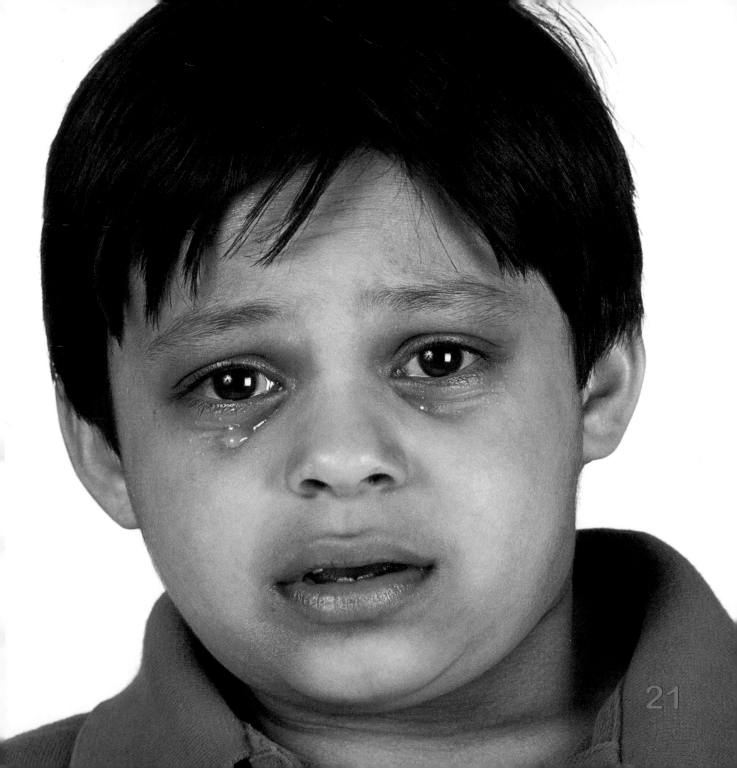

This is what I look like when I am sad.

Words to Know

eyebrow

eyelids

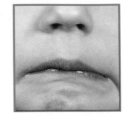

frown

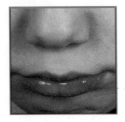

lip

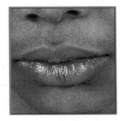

mouth

wrinkle

Index

Web Sites

Due to the changing nature of Internet links, PowerStart Press has developed an online list of Web sites related to the subject of this book. This site is updated regularly. Please use this link to access the list:

www.powerkidslinks.com/llafe/sad/